TRIUMPH TRIDENT

THE BEST PRODUCTION RACER EVER

ROY MADDOX

AMBERLEY

First published 2019

Amberley Publishing
The Hill, Stroud,
Gloucestershire, GL5 4EP

www.amberley-books.com

ISBN: 978 1 4456 7851 1 (print)
ISBN: 978 1 4456 7852 8 (ebook)

British Library Cataloguing in Publication Data.
A catalogue record for this book is available from the British Library.

Typeset in 10pt on 13pt Celeste.
Typesetting by Aura Technology and Software Services, India.
Printed in the UK.

Contents

Introduction

It is important that the reader understands that I am not an expert on the Triples, but as a motorcyclist for over fifty years I have always had a passion for this iconic motorcycle. I hope that you will consider this book as an introduction to the Triples and encourage you to investigate in greater depth.

It would have been impossible for me to create this book without the support of many friends and Triple owners. In particular my sincere thanks go to John Young, whose archive and Posh Garage Archive I have exploited to the fullest degree. I also thank John for his permission to photograph his motorcycles and to use the photographs he provided, including various drawings.

While I produced many of the photographs myself, other illustrations have been provided by Dick Sleath, Graeme Cook, Frank Marshall, Kelvin Munson, Piet Andrianns and Rod Hale, and I thank them for their support and permission.

Special thanks go to Craig Vetter, who provided material not previously seen and granted me permission to use it in this book. I would also like to acknowledge his unique contribution to the history of the motorcycle.

Every attempt has been made to seek permission for copyright material used in this book. However, if I have inadvertently used copyright material without permission/acknowledgement I apologise and will make the necessary correction at the first opportunity.

I hope you enjoy this book and learn something new, and that you are encouraged to explore the Triumph Trident T150 and BSA Rocket 3 after reading.

Roy Maddox
Hinckley
2019

RESERVED
TRIUMPH
TRIDENT
PARKING
ONLY
TRIUMPH
TRIUMPH
TRIUMPH

Big Triple Blockbuster

The story of the Triumph/BSA Triples is such that if it were the screen play for a Hollywood film, it would be rejected as an unbelievable fantasy. The Triple legend started in the early

TRIUMPH TRIDENT

Some two months prior to the Island I had begun to wonder about the machines, think about them incessantly, and, after the inevitable nagging to Triumph's PRO, Ivor Davies, to anticipate. Silly schoolboy-at-the-end-of-term type anticipation, tinged with a barely subdued sense of expectant excitement.

My heart was sinking as I arrived at Triumph's doorstep. A steady river of people was overflowing from the place, and winding its way to bus stops, trains and traffic jams. I had been told that someone would "wait up" for me, but then I had been told this before on other occasions by other people and had been greeted by empty silence. I saw a wink of chrome and purple, waiting outside the advertising department, in the mellowing wateriness of the evening sun. Someone was indeed waiting up for me, and worries evaporated as I let the machine seep into all four corners of my eyeballs. It looked promising. No – it looked a damn sight more than that. It looked downright delicious. I won't say that it was the most handsome machine in the world, but I will say that it pleased me visually as no other machine has ever done. It even went so far as to oust Laverda from my personal number one eye-feast. The battleship lines of 1970's model had gone. There had been an ageing process, but in reverse – from the paunchy bulging of a replete middle age to the lithe grace of maturing youth. It was still unmistakeably the same machine, but without excess flabbiness and ungainliness. Side panels had been refined down, and blended into the sweep of the now mono coloured tank.

The Heath Robinson, jet-propelled sardine can silencers had waffled their last goodbye, and their position had been usurped by the slimly tapering megaphone type which feature on the majority of the Triumph/Beesa twins. The front mudguard on the new model looked to me an inch or so shorter (rearwards) than of yore. Not the most inspired move practically, but together with the mudguard's less prominent bracing of thick but resilient wire and the Ceriani looking forks (so no gaiters), it slimmed down the entire front end and lightened it on the eye. The forks sweep uninterrupted from spindle to yoke, uncluttered by the punctuation of the old headlight brackets. Again, thick wire suffices ably for suspending the lighting department.

But the styling which caused more stir more often in the Isle of Man were the hubs. They've been conical for some time now, as the whole world knows. Now, though, they are fabricated from polished alloy and, believe me, they sparkle. Up at the front, the black enamel of that extraordinary brakeplate, with its evergawping mouth of a ventilator, contrasted to strikingly good effect with the glitter of the hub, somehow giving the front end added definition.

"Horse power."

The overall impression was not the hewn-from-one-piece-of-metal impression that one gains from a Honda Four, No. Nevertheless it was a stolid, solid package exuding a massive and taught gracefulness. As no other 'bike I've yet ridden, it crooked a calculating forefinger at one and beckoned, begged, and finally demanded you to ride it hard, fast and long. It doesn't require any particularly subtle imagination to gather that I liked it as much – more in fact – than I thought I would. Again that old familiar tingle, and I hadn't even sat on the thing yet.

The key was pressed into my hand and I was pointed down the road towards London. Immediately everything felt "right". Within 500 yards I had been riding the machine for years. Familiarity came upon me so rapidly as to be startling. I generally adapt quickly to gear positions and which side does what, but this was ridiculous. The engine note was pure, even comical, delight. Ticking over at 500 rpm, the thing would gurgle away happily to itself like a full fed baby before sleep. Gently pull the wire and the gurgle would become a deep, rounded belly laugh, full of mellow richness. Raise the three slides a little more, make the heart beat a little faster, and the note rose to a hollow, throaty moan. Open the thing fully and it was a stomach twitching wail of some unseen, though benevolent spirit. Sounds are the next most evocative things to smells. For me, the sound of the Trident being warmed to its task in the early morning, evokes the Island and the atmosphere of race week. It's as simple and as logical as that.

The engine was still tight, a mere 300 miles had passed under the T.T.100s. It was only the immediate sympathy that I had with the motor which enabled me to complete the 100 odd miles from Meriden at a sedate 60 mph.

Motorways at their hideous best are tedious, and are good for one thing and one thing only. And obviously a new engine precluded any of that. So the journey was spent in sedate sightseeing, neck craning from left to right, with the odd, obligatory glance forward. One thing already stood out – the seating position. It was, for my six and a bit feet, superb. Feet rested an inch or so forward of a lateral line from the nose of the saddle; brake and gear levers required no jiggery-pokery to cover or snick at. And the 'bars were perhaps the most sensible I have yet ridden with, producing a comfortable and entirely adequate combination for either threading the needle in town traffic, or, as I was to learn later, high speed cruising – and I don't mean a steady 70 either. They minimised "sail" effect and the resulting wander when a 100 mph breeze tugged at both sleeves. Seating wasn't the softest, but it seemed to break in during my 1600 miles with the Trident.

Dawn had cracked an ignominious number of hours prior to my leaving for Liverpool the next morning. Motorcycles seem to shrink into insignificance when seen against the background of a long journey. Most provide a precarious island of motion when thought of as a mere means of conveyance. A totally personal view, the product even of an ever realistic imagination. But setting out on that warm and slightly muggy morning I felt staid, comfortable, and utterly confident that the machine would see me through whatever I threw at it, whenever I chose to throw it. And, once more, I can but put this assurance down to a sixth sense – a prescience if you like. Sling at me that sitting on top of seven hundred quid's worth of new bicycle I damn well ought to feel "staid, comfortable and confident" and I'll reply smuggly that I merely write what I felt.

By the time Birmingham (Jewel of the Midlands) was fast approaching, the engine felt loose enough to be cruised at a steady 80. You will find it as hard to believe as I did that not one single motorcycle passed me at that speed. Don't come wailing to Aldwych House that you cruised your Grommet-Bloggs Special all the way to Liverpool at a steady 120. You probably did, naughty boy, you just weren't in my vicinity when you were doing it. And don't misunderstand me. I'm not holding myself up as the paragon of the hard, fast and hairy riding motorcyclist. But on the return journey, where the boredom of the whole thing could only be alleviated by getting it over and done with as quickly as possible, the only machines who tramped on with me at a steady 30 or 35 miles per hour in excess of the limit were a couple of Scandinavians on big Hondas and Kawasakis. Perhaps these worthy gents didn't really want to leave their companions on slower machinery, but I do know that they didn't maintain their speed for very long. When I say a steady cruising speed I mean the simple process of maintaining a given velocity over, perhaps 100 miles or so, not a thirty mile blast after which rider and machine sigh and gently fall back to the legal limit.

Perhaps motorcycles reflect the mentality of their owners. But I do know that, as I took the machine for a leisurely chunter round-the course, the die of deep affection that I felt for the Trident was well and truly set. Come the following afternoon, Sunday, and another circuit

46

44

There have probably been more articles written about the Triples than any other model over the years.

1960s with the gem of an idea and continues to this day with brand-new racing Triples still being produced to order. The history of the Triple road bikes is intrinsically linked to their racing success on circuits around the world. When sales stalled it was victories in prestigious races that helped turn sales around both in the UK and the US. Those victories became the stuff of legend and Triple riders became household names regardless of which side of the pond they lived.

It should be understood that at that time production motorcycle racing was more popular than Grand Prix racing and every manufacturer worked hard to achieve success with machines that anyone could buy from their local bike dealership. Against the might of the fully funded and sponsored Japanese and European race teams the Triples amassed victory after victory in the Isle of Man TT, the Spa 24 hour race and Daytona in the US. This unique machine even gave birth to its own race series, originally called the Match Races and later the Transatlantic Races, where the best riders from America and Britain raced around British circuits, entertaining massive crowds on Triumph and BSA Triples.

Track success directly led to improved sales and from a bike few wanted the Triples became a must-have machine – a status that continues into the twenty-first century. The unparalleled success on the track and on-road mastery have led to the Triples reaching the position of a two-wheeled icon and lion in the classic bike jungle.

Having set the opening scenes for our Hollywood blockbuster, let us now examine the world in which this tale is set. The two main places were Meriden (Triumph) and Umberslade Hall (BSA), a few miles apart in the Midlands of the UK.

Why a Triple?

The mid-1960s hold a unique position in the history of two-wheeled motorised vehicles. Numerous events are labelled pre-65 to indicate that the event is for riders of machines constructed before 1965, but why? Simply the middle of the decade marked the insurgence of Japanese motorcycles into the West's market place. What followed was a complete restructuring of the motorcycle industry – particularly in Britain, where its decline from this point was rapid.

I would like you to suspend reality for a second time and ask you to consider the impact that would have been made in the British motorcycle industry and with the bike-buying public if the Triumph Trident 750 T150 had been launched in 1966 or earlier. At that time British riders were faced with 500 and 650 Twins, a few 350s and a 450 Twin from Japan.

In this suspension of reality the Triples would have been a firm hit for the manufacturers and could have reinforced their position as the pre-eminent performance brands. Even in 1968 it was the fastest motorcycle in the world, faster even than the first Honda 750/4s. Imagine that kind of performance two years (or earlier) ahead of the big Honda. In this alternative reality a whole industry would have been refreshed but, as time revealed, it took another thirty years before the Triumph Triple singlehandedly rescued the British motorcycle industry under the stewardship of John Bloor in Hinckley, Leicestershire.

The tale of the Triumph Trident and the BSA Rocket 3 is one of the most interesting and yet frustrating in all the annals of classic British motorcycles; frustrating because it took so many years to get from concept idea to prototype and then to production. The pre-Honda 750/4 window of opportunity had closed.

A compact Triple engine was the answer to a replacement for the successful Twins, which were reaching the limit of both reliability and performance.

The Triumph Trident T150 was launched with a new look that did not have many fans in the factory or with the public. Here, the T150 wears the famous Windjammer fairing designed by Craig Vetter.

The general perception is that the Triples are 'a Daytona-and-a-half', meaning that they were based on the 500 Twin with one more cylinder added. This is basically incorrect. Like the Daytona, the bore and stroke on the unit-construction 500s was slightly over square at 69 mm X 65.5 mm, but the Triples' bore and stroke was slightly under square at 67 mm X 70 mm, which it shares not with the Triumph 500 Twin, but with Triumph's 250 single-cylinder line, the TR25.

Contemporary knowledge suggests that the 250 single was chosen over the 500 Twin because the smaller bore allowed a narrower engine. Herbert (Bert) Hopwood and Doug Hele had a plan to modularise the entire engine line with 500 Twins, 750 Triples and even a 1,000cc four-cylinder machine, all built from the same basic layout. This modular design was to be based around an 83cc single which would be the foundation of a 249cc Triple. Additionally, their intention was to produce a single overhead cam six-speed road bike and a double overhead cam eight-speed GP racer, but sadly these became more missed opportunities and unfulfilled dreams.

Doug Hele must be considered the father of the Triple in both its road and racing form. Born in 1919, he was forty-three years old when he moved to Triumph as the Chief Development Engineer, a position he held from 1962 to 1973. Hele began his career as an apprentice at the Austin Motor Company at Longbridge, but he was no novice in motorcycle design, previously having working for Douglas, Norton and BSA before joining the 1,800-strong workforce at Meriden.

The final development of the Triple was the T160, which came with improved performance, reliability and modern specification that enabled it to deal with road and track with ease.

As excellent as the Triumph 650 Twins were, the configuration was fast reaching the limits of performance, durability and reliability. Even so, Twins were about to go even faster! Vibration had always been an issue and now it was becoming a problem. As Triumph continued to develop the brand by punching out the old 500cc Tiger T100 to create the 650cc Triumph 6T Thunderbird in 1950, vibration had gotten progressively worse as performance increased. The TR6 with its splayed head in 1956, followed by the twin-carb Bonneville in 1959, did nothing to reduce the vibration problem. Faced with the reintroduction of the engine in unit-construction form to respond to dealers and riders in the US, the need for greater performance was uppermost in the minds of Hopwood and Hele.

They came up with an innovative new idea. Rather than attempting to balance a more powerful big Twin with a 360-degree crank, the big idea was to split power between three cylinders, and array the crankshaft with a piston at every 120 degrees.

The Triple, while to a radical new design, was built along very traditional British lines and similar to Triumph Twin design. It had vertically split cases, a one-piece crank with plain bearings and two cams driven by a gear train on the right, with a primary chain on the left. The tappets, tappet blocks, pushrods, rocker arms and spindles were all right out of Triumph's playbook.

In 1961, there were plenty of Singles and Twins, and even a few Fours, but no Triples! Given the conservative stance of the BSA and Triumph management at the time it was a crazy idea. However, by 1962 plans had been drawn up and by 1965 a running prototype engine in a 650 Bonneville frame had been created.

With details on the drawing board in 1962, production could have commenced in 1963, some five years before the Trident saw the light of day in 1968.

From the day of its launch the Triple had to battle for recognition and race victories. There can be no doubt that the Triples won many of the battles and came out the other side as an iconic British motorcycle, sitting at the top of many riders' want list.

Endless Conflict

Endless conflict within the organisation did nothing to accelerate the launch of the Triple as the project was haunted by perpetual delay. However, it is not that far from the truth that Honda had a greater influence on the project development than either Triumph or BSA. The news of the impending release of the Honda 750/4 forced them into purposeful action and a hasty launch.

After several years of bike shed tinkering with the Triple, it would have been realistic to have expected they would have had something ready for market. Again, frustratingly they were not even close. The internal conflict left BSA slighted by Triumph's popularity and success both on and off the track. They also had a desire to offer their dealers (particularly in the US) something different.

So BSA insisted that the Triple was also made with their badge, but this wasn't going to be a simple badge-engineered clone of the Trident. Instead, the BSA Rocket 3 took all the basic internals and encased them in an entirely new set of engine cases whose only purpose was to provide a 15-degree forward tilt to the cylinders, so that it looked different from the Triumph. They completed the folly by dropping it into an entirely new frame that was completely different from the Triumph unit. Without a doubt this selfish manoeuvring delayed the introduction of the new model; equally as concerning was the considerable increase in costs it produced.

The origin of the Triple idea goes back a number of years to 1961, when Bert Hopwood produced a plan for a 750cc Triple motorcycle as a possible solution to the increasing problem of vibration on the company's Twins as performance improved. The concept was further enhanced when Doug Hele designed a compact clutch drive assembly that removed another problem of excessive footrest width.

The idea of a Triple seems to have gained momentum when Harry Sturgeon assumed the roles of Marketing Director and Manufacturing Director as the old guard vacated their factory roles. His immediate challenge was to improve the quality of BSA products, which had fallen in previous years. His impact was almost immediate, with turnover increasing by 40 per cent from 1964 to 1966.

Sturgeon had long been keen on a 250cc three-cylinder machine in two guises: a six-gear road model and an eight-gear racer. So he was more receptive to the three-cylinder idea than his predecessors; Edward Turner called the Triple concept 'potty'. With fresh life being given to the Hopwood-Hele partnership, formative development work moved on apace. After twelve months the first Triple engine was produced with 58 bhp at 7,250 rpm. It ran smoothly and was only 40 lbs heavier than the Bonneville power unit. With a cast-iron cylinder block and overall dry weight of 420 lbs, the first Triple bike was ready for production in 1965. Early sales of the Ogle-designed bike were slow and only picked up in 1971, when they returned to a more traditional 'Triumph look'. Again decisions were made that saw income reduced for three years – income that was badly needed to combat Japanese imports and improve production and development.

Above and opposite: Although the original look with a 'bread-bin' tank and 'ray-gun' silencers did not find favour, we now have a more sympathetic view of the 'Ogle Look' today.

A Matter of Design

A Bike to Ogle

Historically both BSA and Triumph had their own team of designers, as was the case for most motorcycle manufacturers worldwide. Uniquely, the Triples started with an in-house creation and then they embraced external design input. The early prototypes followed the 'Triumph look' lineage – a look that was cast aside before being picked up and dusted off for reintroduction as the 'Beauty Kit' and the Vetter 'Top Line' look of the T160. To produce the sought-after 'new look' for the new Triple, BSA/Triumph turned to Ogle Design.

Ogle Design was and remains a British design consultancy company, founded in 1954 by David Ogle and based in Letchworth, Hertfordshire, where it still operates today. Ogle was involved in transport design and small-scale car production.

The founder was killed in a car crash in 1962 and Tom Karen (who had a background in aircraft and washing machine design) took over the lead role in the company, and this resulted in the end of car production. However, Ogle Design built their reputation for industrial design, with responsibility for some British design icons which included one that appeared in a galaxy far, far away:

The Bush TR130/TR82 Portable Radio, launched in 1959
The Chopper bicycle for Raleigh, launched in 1970
The BSA Rocket 3
The Triumph Trident T150
The Reliant Scimitar GTE, launched in 1968
The Bond Bug, launched in 1970
The Reliant Robin, launched in 1973
Plus Truck cabs and coaches
For George Lucas, Luke Skywalker's XP-34 Landspeeder

Skywalker's Landspeeder was constructed around the chassis of a Bond Bug. One of the major challenges the film production crew faced was disguising the wheels to create the illusion that the craft was hovering.

To aid the design project of the Triple, Ogle were provided with a Triple engine with no internals and two frames – one based on the Triumph T120 Bonneville frame and a second based on the BSA A65 lightning frame.

The design brief given to Ogle was that they wanted 'a very flashy American look, like a Cadillac car'. The tank, seat and side panels were squared off. The now familiar 'bread-bin' petrol tank was imagined from taking the Ogle-designed Bush radio and stretching it. Even the BSA badge corresponded to the tuning dial. The infamous ray-gun silencers were added as a joke but were loved when reviewed by the decision-makers back at the factory. Indicators and combined switch gear were also included in the design, although they were rejected by the same people, who thought it was a copy of the Honda 250 Dream and 'they chose the design they disliked least'.

A mock-up machine was ready by March 1967. The plan was that the Triples would be launched at the UK's Motorcycle Show in 1967.

The original Ogle drawings show monobloc carburettors fitted, which indicates that the drawings were made before Amal introduced concentrics in 1966/67. It is therefore realistic to consider that the drawings were produced by Bryon Fitzpatrick and Jim English during 1964/65.

The first drawing shows the earlier version of the silencers with three exit tubes. This was not meant to be a design feature but was included as a bit of fun so a decision about the actual design of the silencers could be made later. Along with the monobloc carburettors an alloy cast down tube is envisaged, which appears very similar to Greeves competition machines. The first idea of the rear light arrangement, however, seems to have stood the test of time.

The second drawing shows further idea development with a fibreglass rear end, the inclusion of a radiator and refinement of the innovative silencer. The drawings illustrate well that ideas like a scalloped seat, silencer design and frame-engine relationship were continually under review, with development being influenced by Far Eastern and Italian bikes. Even with this it is easy to identify the germ of the final Triple design.

Of course the involvement of Ogle Design introduced further delays for the release and the final product was viewed by the public as anything but beautiful. The Triumph Trident and BSA Rocket 3 hit the market with a clunky fuel tank so square that it became known as the 'bread-bin tank' in the UK and the 'shoebox tank' in the USA. A set of slab-like silencers were incorporated into the design and were considered so outlandish they were nicknamed the 'Ray Gun' silencers. Functionally, they worked better than anything that came after and today are considered a must-have for any restoration.

However, because there was to be a distinctive BSA and Triumph version of the Triple, all major castings had to be duplicated, which greatly increased the cost of the project.

Acrimony, distrust and stubbornness produced radical styling that failed to do the bike justice and was disliked and despised by many. In those early days the styling cost the Triples a great many sales, at a time when they needed to gain market acceptance and share quickly. Poor styling can make or break any product and good styling should not cost any more than the poor styling. By the time they got the styling right it was too late and the window of opportunity had closed. In a desperate move Triumph introduced the beauty kit, which was provided through dealers. The kits could be dealer-installed or installed by the owner and went a long way toward fixing the questionable styling, particularly in America. The rushed-to-market kits included a new teardrop tank (reflecting the established Triumph style), new convex side panels and a new set of conventional silencers.

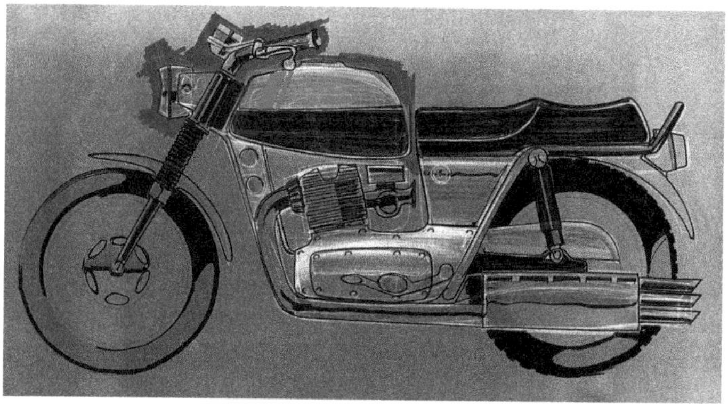

Above and opposite: The original Ogle Design drawings show various external influences. Clearly, as their first motorcycle project, the designers reviewed current trends and it is easy to identify Japanese and Italian influences. However, the Greeves alloy influence is a little surprising – maybe the designer watched scrambling on *World of Sport*.

The basis for the Vetter design was the Rocket 3, which had tremendous success on race circuits in the 1970s, and even today they are a racing weapon.

In a last throw of the dice, American Craig Vetter (creator of the Windjammer fairing) was asked to design something special to boost sales in the US. Vetter took the stodgy BSA and restyled it completely with a flowing new one-piece tank/seat unit that flowed into an integrated rear mudguard. The unit was made from polyester resin and was held in place over the steel tank by a new product called 'Velcro'.

The paint scheme was both original and pleasing to the eye, with bright orange and a striking yellow stripe. The front forks were extended, as was the trend with the contemporary Chopper practice. The bike was further enhanced with an extra ¾ inches added to cylinder engine fins and an impressive set of three upswept exhaust pipes that ran along the right side of the bike. The X75 Hurricane (A75 BSA originally) was stunning and remains today an icon of its type and generation. It all flowed together like nothing anyone had ever seen before. The tiny petrol tank and narrow tank to seat 'waist' had the sex appeal to be a real hit but was impractical for any owner wanting to cover distance. Production of this beautifully different motorcycle ran for a single year and it sold in relatively small numbers.

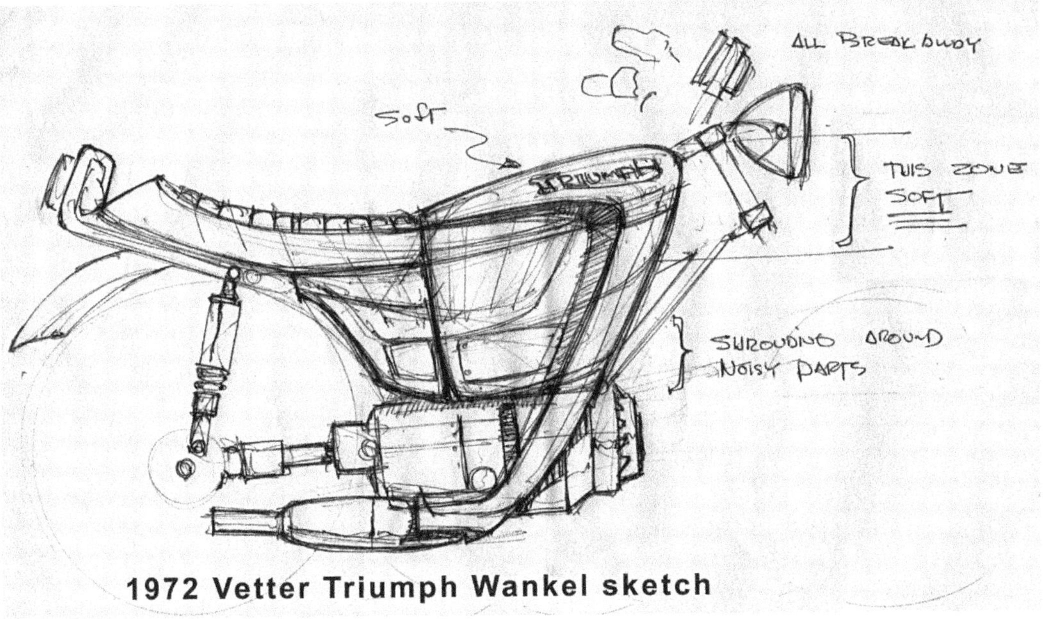

Craig used a simple pen and paper for his design drafts. Here he imagines a Wankel-engined Triumph.

The Hurricane illustrates the first production appearance of 'The Vetter Top Line'. His vision went on to influence a generation of motorcycles.

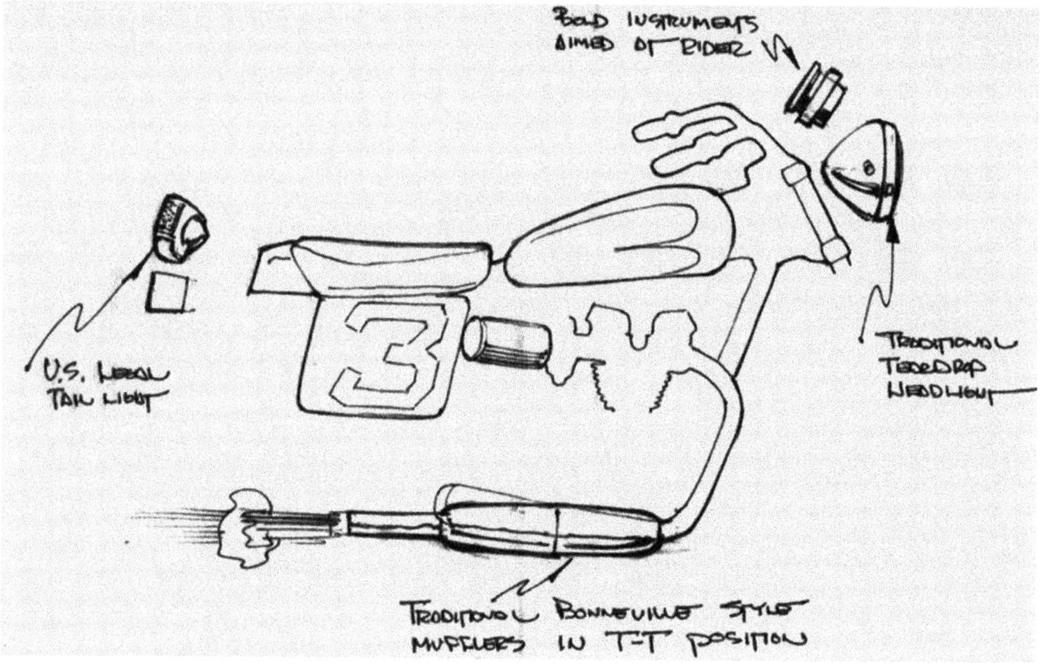

Development drawing of Vetter Bonneville TT.

Don Brown conceived of the X75 Hurricane project and had certain design principles in mind, which he conveyed to Craig Vetter. It was a secret project funded from petty cash on a weekly basis. While Don worked with Craig at the outset, he claimed no credit for the concept or styling of the Hurricane; he was happy to acknowledge these lay solely with Craig. No one at the BSA Group was told about the project, and certainly not any of his American colleagues. Only three members of staff were told about it and they were instructed not to discuss it with anyone except each other.

Craig Vetter agreed to do the job as the styling engineer. He also agreed to be paid weekly for materials used and expenses for his assistant only. He was to keep track of his time and, should the styling ever be accepted by the factory and eventually put into production, he was to be paid at the rate of $15 per hour, according to Craig himself. Once an agreement was reached Craig was provided with the keys to a Rocket 3 (engine number KC-00197 A75R), believed to be one of the Rocket 3s that had just set speed and long-distance records at Daytona.

The genius approached the design challenge in a refreshingly imaginative and innovative way, identifying the importance of the relationship between aesthetics of motorcycle design and the female form, which became known as the 'Vetter Top Line'. Let's let Craig Vetter himself explain:

> My "Top Line" was the result of a talk with Felix Kalinski on 10 October 1972. He had been at Triumph since May and could see that my designs were consistent, recognizable and Triumph. It was important, too, that he already recognized the "family look" of my designs.

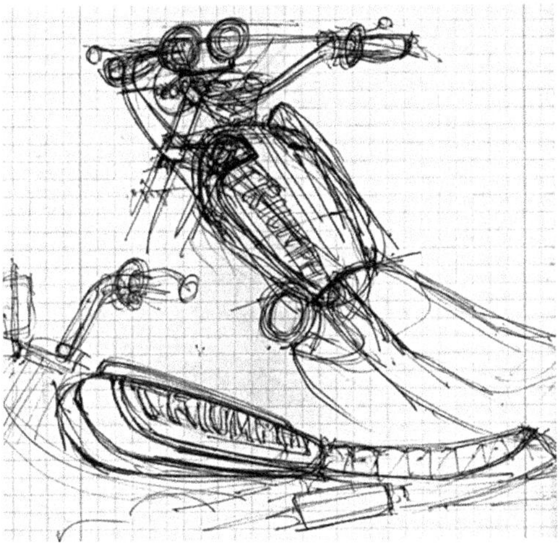

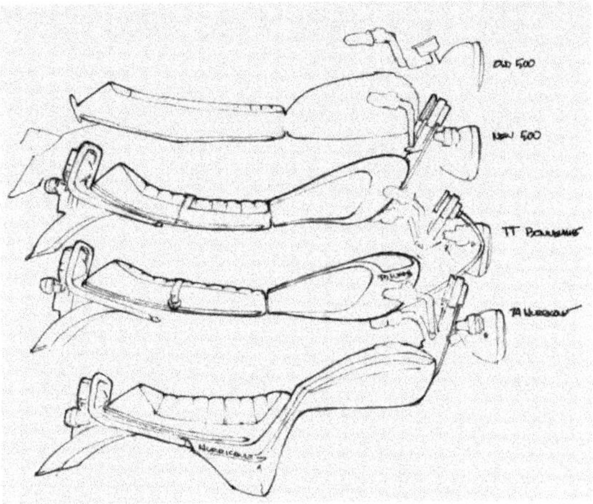

1972 Vetter Top Line on all Triumphs

Above and below: Development drawings of 'The Vetter Top Line' and the Hurricane.

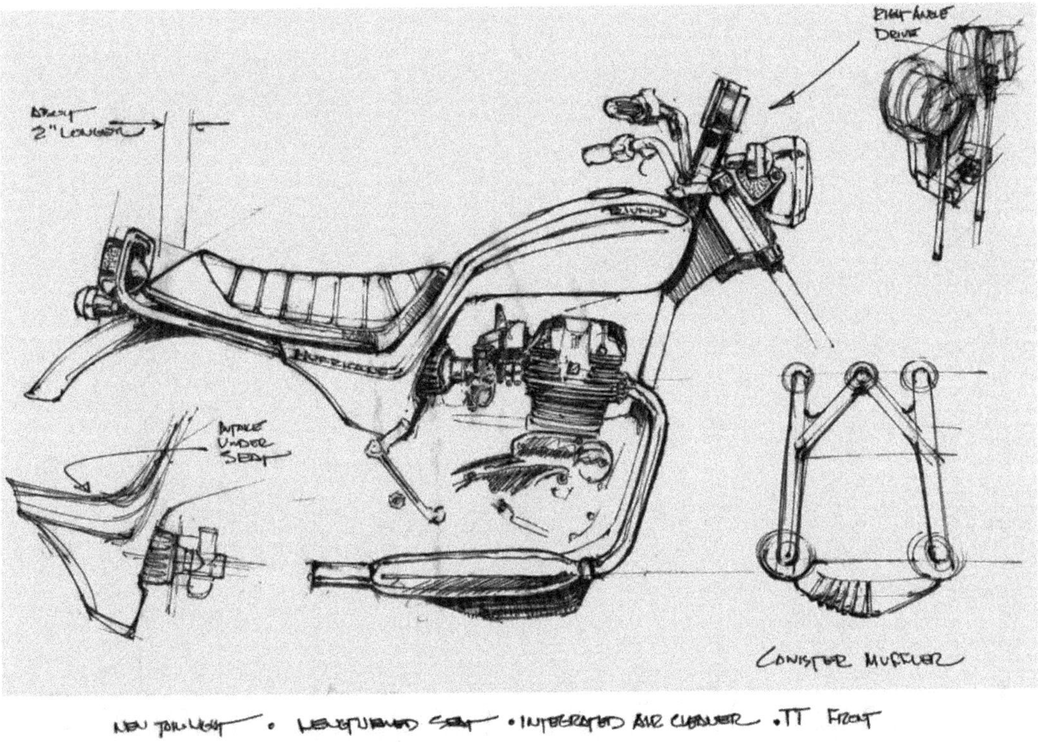

But my designs included more: they were "American", too, which added a new flavour. I had just turned thirty and my designs were "svelte" like a lady.

All my designs of the day – my fairings and Triumph motorcycles – had the attractiveness of a pretty girl because I associated girls with motorcycles. It seemed that the British associated motorcycles with road racing while we Americans associated them with girls.

First applied to Craig Vetter's Bonneville TT, his 'Top Line' became the new 'Triumph look'. The 1972 Bonneville TT was supposed to replace the high-frame Bonneville, but it became the Triumph T160 of 1975 instead.

Yet again, BSA managed to turn potential into failure. BSA's mounting internal problems delayed launch of the BSA A75 Hurricane so long that when it was finally released, BSA was no longer selling motorcycles, so it had to be rebadged as a Triumph X75 Hurricane.

In test this stunning Triple failed to meet the requirements to pass new noise laws in the US. Just 1,152 Triumph Hurricanes were built (1973 model year only), making this not only one of the most exciting classic British motorcycles, but also one of the rarest.

Craig Vetter exploits pen and paper to record his design ideas.

The final creation, the 1973 Hurricane X-75 (TRX75) – an extraordinary design that struggled to sell initially, but which is now one of the most sought-after British motorcycles.

Craig Vetter examines his design for the Bonneville TT.

A promotional information sheet, part of the media pack used at the launch of the 1973 Hurricane.

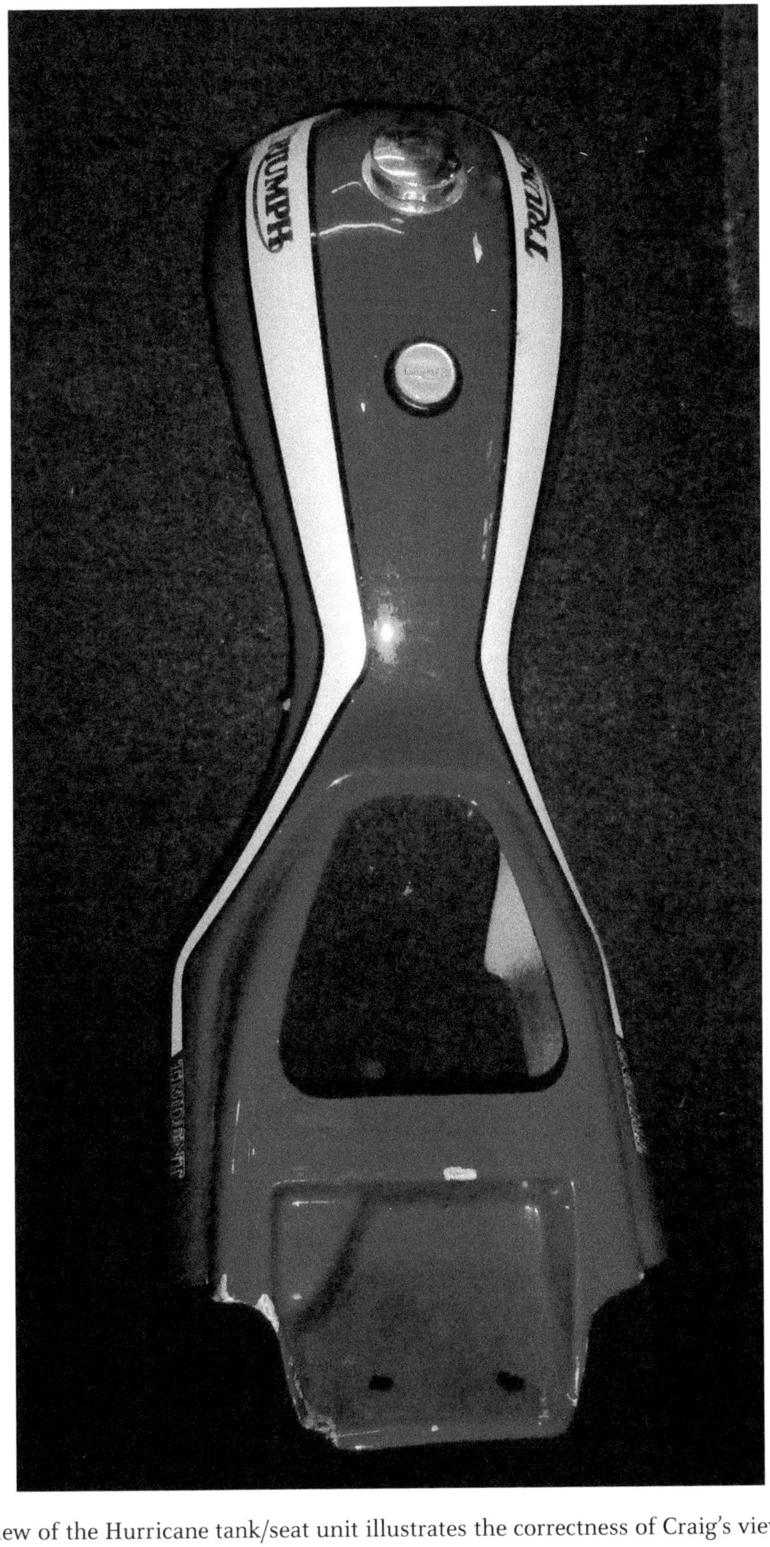

This view of the Hurricane tank/seat unit illustrates the correctness of Craig's view that a motorcycle should mimic the female form.

Pre-Production

The Triple took physical shape in late 1964 with the factory code P1 (Project One) and later P2. In January 1965 the engine was tested on a dynamotor and found to produce 59.5 bhp – a 15 per cent improvement over the Bonneville. Fuel was controlled by three Amal monobloc carburettors with chopped bowls so they fit in the tight space available. The centre carburettor was fitted with a high-flow needle usually used when alcohol was utilised to allow increased fuel volume.

Testing identified issues like overheating, distortion between the cast-iron cylinder and alloy head and wet sumping. Early fault correction to produce a functioning engine was implemented by Experimental Department fitter Harry Woolridge.

Track days like the VMCC's Festival of Thousand Bikes at Mallory Park always sees a contingent of road and race Triples.

In 1966, while England was producing fireworks by winning the Football World Cup, Doug Hele produced his own pyrotechnics when the prototype Triple machine he was riding burst into flame. Quick action by a passing fellow biker meant little damage was inflicted.

During the same year the secret Triple prototype was taken to the MIRA testing facilities and demonstrated to police forces. The smoothness of the 120-degree phasing crank was remarked on positively.

P1 fulfilled its intended function and led the way to P2, which included major changes. It was given the shorter stroke of 67 x 70 mm, reflecting the C15 start 250 modular idea. The 4 mm bore increase allowed bigger valves to be used which, with the alloy cylinder block and revised push rod tube arrangement, improved cooling substantially.

More robust main bearings, a redesigned lubrication system and relocation of the oil pump improved cooling and reliability. The introduction of a Triplex Renold chain primary drive reduced noise while the multi-plate/multi-spring clutch was replaced with a single-plate diaphragm-spring Borg & Beck unit.

By mid-1966 three P2s were on the road and being tested by riders Percy Tait and Tony Lomax in two forms: the T150 Triumph and the A75 Tri Star BSA, later to be renamed the Rocket 3.

There is little doubt that the original Triple was only intended to be a stopgap for five years while a whole new line of modern OHC and DOHC machines were created at the infamous Umberslade Hall.

So, rather than invest substantial development funds on a whole new design with horizontally split cases, they decided to keep tooling costs to a minimum by employing as much of the twin-cylinder engine tooling and production techniques as possible.

Thus, the vertically split cases remained. However, rather than with two like the Twins, the Trident was 'blessed' with three, with a centre case carrying the two centre main bearings and two outer cases, each with an end bearing. This was an overcomplicated assembly which had no less than seven castings and many vertical seams that were prone to oil leaks, which would have been removed by horizontally split cases. Using old tools and techniques involving numerous time-consuming processes slowed initial production to about fifty engines per week in total at BSA's Small Heath plant, and the engines were shared between Triumph and BSA. The complexity of the whole process can be illustrated when it is realised that it required fifty-six stages along with forty-eight jigs and fixtures simply to machine the centre section of the crankcase.

We know that the Triumph and BSA engines were slightly different, which meant they were totally different on the assembly line. The crankshaft, however, was a real work of art. As a product of BSA's own forge, it was produced in one piece with all three shafts in line. It was then heated and twisted until the shafts were set at 120 degrees from each other. After BSA sold off assets in a vain effort to survive, Triples received conventionally made forged crankshafts from an outside source. Sadly, the unique triple-cylinder design was at its birth both new and obsolete at the same time. The ancient pushrod engine dated back to Edward Turner's Speed Twin of 1938. However, it was still an impressive construction that produced pleasing power and handling. Even so, the Triple's biggest problem was sloppy build quality from the factory during a time of great upheaval in the BSA-Triumph empire. When these niggles were

Triumph Trident T150.

BSA Rocket 3.

subsequently sorted, either by a dealer or the owner, they proved to be very fast, sturdy and dependable machines. Modern owners have the benefit of a legion of parts, upgrades and techniques that go a long way towards solving those historical problems and shortcomings that have troubled the Triples. Regardless of the conflict and issues, the Triples are perhaps the best classic British motorcycle ever built, producing a sound like no other!

Trident and Rocket 3 pre-production prototypes were known as P2 machines to differentiate from the original P1, which had been constructed during late 1967 and early 1968. The pre-fix construction of P2 'Engine Number' first appeared on 27 June 1967 and continued until 1 August 1967. A specific group of four prototype machines were transported to California for testing. The trials went well and the only major change in bike spec was the replacement of the Dunlop ribbed front tyre with the new Dunlop K70. Consequently, production commenced in July 1968.

The pending launch of the Honda CB 740-4 catapulted Triumph/BSA to commence production of the Triples rather than any long-term planning.

The Triples are Launched

Right from the outset the Trident was aimed at the lucrative American market, but from the 1968 launch sales did not take off due to bad timing with the arrival of the Honda CB750/4, questionable styling and suspect build quality. Equally, sales were hampered by low production figures; initially only about 2,500 units were constructed per year and there was a high US price (a 1971 Trident sold for $1,765, while a 1971 Norton Commando sold for $1,490 and a Honda CB750/4 for $1,495). So into this environment the Triples were

launched at the Brands Hatch race circuit on Thursday 3 April 1969, followed the next day by the first public appearance of the Triple at the Brighton Show.

Over their seven-year run the Triumph Trident and BSA Rocket 3 only achieved a combined production total of 27,480 machines.

For the owner problems commenced even before riding due to the starting routine, as the engine had to be kicked into life since no electric starter was fitted. This method of starting harked back to the 1950s and meant that the float was held down with two outside ticklers, which drenched the owner's gloves and the engine with petrol. Other historical elements included a four-speed gearbox and drum brakes, which all helped to produce a Triple that was old-fashioned at its launch.

Despite all the problems and the disappointing sales, the Triple was one spectacular motorcycle. It was fast – very fast – winning races and achieving great success. Triples won the legendary Isle of Man production TT races for six consecutive years from 1970 through to 1975 (and the Formula 750 TT race in 1971 and 1972) – a stunning achievement by any measure. At that time the Japanese were making a major onslaught on all forms of motorcycle sport. Add to that the financial condition of both BSA and Triumph as companies, and the level of success that they accomplished was truly amazing.

Among classic motorcycles the Triples have every attribute to cope with modern roads and traffic. Many owners see their Triples as motorcycles to ride on the road and on the track rather than ornaments.

What the Papers Said

The first public road test of the Triples was carried by Dutch motorcycle magazine *Motor* in September 1968. As well as a road test by the journalist and author Mick Woollett there was also the first Triple advertisement, promoting the virtues of this new unique machine. The bike tested, SAC 341G, was clearly produced as a road test bike as it appeared two months later in British bike magazine *Motorcycle Sport*.

This was not the first report of the Triple however. That honour went to Dutch magazine *Motorsport*. Along with photos of the three-cylinder in-line engine, it also reported that in 1966 the bike had been tested at Brands Hatch.

As early as October 1968, America's *Cycle World* announced on their cover 'The World's First Test'. The coverage was much more detailed than the Dutch magazine and contained opinions and statistics to inform its readers, stating accurately: 'There is not another three-cylinder roadster motorcycle in production.'

Under test a top speed of 117.03 mph was recorded and the quarter mile was covered in 13.028 seconds, which was improved upon after adjustments, achieving 102.73 mph at the end of the quarter. It identified that three 27 mm Amal Concentrics were fitted and in the language of the time stated revealingly: 'A groovy looking 0.25pt capacity oil cooler is mounted beneath the nose of the fuel tank.'

The price was said to be $1,760. Interestingly, however, it was many months before UK road tests gave a purchase price, and when they did it was £615.

The road tester described his experience as: 'Exotic sensation ... The brakes are not up to the task of halting this 500 lb projectile ... The Triumph Trident is a big, fast ground shaker of a motorcycle and there isn't another bike like it!'

The switch to a traditional 'Triumph look' had a positive impact on sales and public perception.

In both November and December 1968 *Motorcycle Sport* magazine carried reports about the Triples and, surprisingly, still had not discovered the purchase price. Readers were provided with fuel consumption figures of 32/34 mpg. Additional information included: 'Triple carbs are linked to a crank assembly which is worked by a single cable.' The exhaust system was referred to as 'Triamised' because the term three-into-two had not been coined at that time. Readers were also informed that the Trident had a single-frame down tube, while the BSA, with its engine sloping forward, had a duplex down tube.

While the coverage by *Motorcycle Sport* was generally positive, it could not resist taking a little swipe at the Triple, probably after experiencing the opposition: 'We think it is a pity that the first new British machine for an age has to be so old fashioned.'

Time seems to have mellowed reports and soon there was a more positive theme to reports and road tests.

In January 1969, *Motorcycle Sport* carried a feature on the Triple for the third month in a row, with its reporting becoming more positive: 'It puts us back on top ... Yes, a tiger and a half ... Civilised travel to the best standards ... Night riding was enjoyable.'

In July 1969 *Cycle* in the US reported that BSA had hired the Daytona Tri-Oval race circuit for the testing of a BSA Rocket 3 ridden by Yvon DuHamel, Dick Mann and Ray Hempstead, during which they tested the bike to its limits.

Piloted by DuHamel, the Rocket 3 covered the first 100 miles at an average of 125.99 mph. A further 50 miles was clocked at 125.72 mph average and over four hours, including a refuelling, an average of 117.545 mph was achieved.

After changing the rear sprocket for a fifty-tooth substitute the top speed was pushed to 128 mph and the hour record to 127.615. By the end of the day and steady adjustments the BSA Rocket 3 was timed at 131.790 mph, making it the fastest production motorcycle in the world.

In the same month the two BSA distributors in the US offered a $25,000 prize for Triples setting records at Bonneville Salt Flats.

The radical new British Triple hit the scene with its sibling wearing the bread-bin/shoebox petrol tank that somehow looked better on the BSA and Ray Gun silencers, entering the marketplace just months ahead of the game-changing Honda 750/4.

Racing Development

Following the launch of the Triples in 1968 sales were not really taking off, particularly in the lucrative American market. In 1969, despite positive press reviews, sales in America only reached 7,000 compared with a very healthy 30,000 for Honda's CB750/4, introduced at the same time. In an effort to boost flagging sales it was decided to mount a racing campaign to highlight the performance and reliability of the Triples.

Given the high profile and success of the current MotoGP series of today, it is difficult to imagine that it was any other way. However, in the late 1960s and early 1970s Grand Prix racing was going through something of poor spell, with poor competition and diminishing interest. It was production motorcycle racing that stepped up to fill the vacuum for both spectators and factories.

For the manufacturers, production racing offered a less expensive way to go racing and an opportunity to generate publicity and media interest in their products. Meanwhile, spectators were treated to machines they could relate to and potentially buy from their local motorcycle showroom.

Triple Dirt Track Racing

However, it was in early 1969 that the first racing Triples took to the racing circuits. In that year the new Triples were not legal to race in AMA Road Racing events in the US, but they were eligible for the newly introduced 'C' Class Formula for 750cc displacement engines in the dirt track discipline. With a weight some 50 lbs heavier than the 650 Triumph Twins it was going to be difficult to get them 'sideways'. This didn't deter local engine tuner Cliff Guild and mechanic Ted Rivard from producing dirt track machines. Two were created: one with a rigid 650 Triumph racing frame for Larry Palmgren and a swing arm Trackmaster frame for Gary Nixon.

The unproven Triples were taken to the National Dirt Track Oval in Nazareth, Pennsylvania, and in practice Nixon did a lap in 43 seconds at a speed of 94 mph, which pleased the team until the Harley KR Twins arrived and clocked a 42-second lap.

Before 1970 was out the Triples were recalled for dirt track duty in the USA again. The choice of frames was repeated with the ever popular Trackmaster for Gary Nixon and the

Above and below: Early photographs of Triples used as regular transport. The bikes proved to be effective, practical machines if well maintained.

Above and below: This BSA Triple replica pays homage to the dirt track bikes ridden by the likes of Jim Rice. The engine has a car-type distributor. The machine was created by Richard Darby and owned by John Young.

Rob North Highboy road race version for Don Castro. The return to the fifty-lap Nazareth National site of the earlier defeat saw a marked improvement with Nixon running second ahead of Castro, both following Chuck Palmgren's winning 650 Yamaha Twin. The only victory recorded by a Triple in an AMA National Dirt Track race was by Jim Rice and his Rocket 3 at the Sedalia, Missouri Mile bringing the Triples involvement in dirt track racing to an end.

Road Racing

Until they were legal for AMA production, road racing class Triples competed at major club events. The Big D Triumph Racing Team from Dallas, Texas, won the American Cycle Association 12 Hour Production GP at Willow Springs, covering 1,001 miles on a road-legal Trident at an average speed of 83.4 mph, beating Honda 4s, Norton Commandos and Kawasaki H1s.

Back in the UK, Triumph decided to take the fullest advantage of production racing.

Triumph Twins had a very successful racing heritage, with model names reflecting that success: e.g. Bonneville and Daytona. In 1969 Malcolm Uphill set a 100 mph lap for a production bike aboard his Triumph at the Tourist Trophy on the Isle of Man. The factory's success with the racing Bonnevilles was used to develop the Triple racers. Cycle parts were easily transferred, as was the improved Quaife racing five-speed gearbox. The Twins had reached the limit of their development and the Triples were about to deliver reliable power at a level unimaginable from the Twins. With the road Triples pushing out 58 bhp reliably, the racing team quickly attained 70 bhp of useable power, which realised 150 mph on the Isle of Man. The engineers Les Williams and Doug Hele sought to create a bike that produced competition-beating output that would be successful in the hands of a racer for the length of the 37.5-mile race of the Manx circuit.

To comply with production racing regulations the Triples were fitted with 27 mm Amal concentric carburettors – the same as the road bike. However, later rubber-mounted 32 mm carburettors from the same manufacturer were fitted by the race team.

It was generally thought that the best upgrade for the racer was the use of a substantial 250 mm double-sided Twin leading-shoe Fontana front brake that did a great job of reducing forward momentum from 150 mph for the heavy Triple

To improve handling, both the front and rear suspension was upgraded. Dunlop had launched the TT100 tyre and provided 19-inch examples rather than the usual 18-inch ones. This had the added advantage of improving the ground clearance on what was a big and low bike. The super dimensions of *Slippery Sam* had no equal for width and length. The rider was protected by a massive fairing that made it ideal for multi-lap races around the Isle of Man. The mass of the Triple also had a problem of grounding on the island despite the bigger tyres. The Heath Robinson solution was to fit the metal bumpers from an old Fiat between the engine and the voluptuous fairing, and this removed the impact of the grounding.

Another element that proved to perform much better than expected was the Ray Gun silencers. Although almost universally disliked by the public, on the racers they were efficient and complimented the power of the three-cylinder engine perfectly.

Above and below: Two racing Triples housed in the Triumph Visitor Experience, Hinckley, Leicestershire, as part of the Triumph factory. Visitors can see a range of displays both historical and right up to date. There is a smart café and shop and factory visits can also be booked.

The production TT was the premier race and the challenge was taken up by the Triples in June 1970. While other teams had sponsorship – John Player cigarettes supported the Norton team – the Triumph operation was more piecemeal, and some may say unprofessional, but then Triumph had a better bike, which after all is what racing is about.

Triumph's campaign was a resounding success, with Malcolm Uphill winning the race ahead of Norton-mounted Peter Williams and Ray Pickrell at a speed of 97.71 mph. Tom Dickie was fourth and the BSA Triple with Bob Heath aboard finished fifth in the 188.65-mile race. Two Honda CB750s ridden by Tommy Robb and John Cooper finished eighth and ninth respectively.

On return to the factory the frame was raised by 1⅜ inches to combat the grounding issue. Before the year was out the improved Triples were back on the track in the famous Bol d'Or 24 Hour race at Montlhéry near Paris. Tom Dickie and Paul Smart covered 469 laps

Controlling the excitement of preparing to race a Triple.

and 1,838 miles at an average speed of 75.553 mph, piloting the Triple to a win by eight laps. It was not this outstanding success beating both Honda and Laverda factory teams that grabbed the headlines, however; that honour went to a Triumph Trident mounted by Percy Tait and Steve Jolly, although they finished in fifth place. Their bike was affected badly when the usual Duckhams 20/50 multigrade oil was changed to an R-grade racing oil. The engine failed to scavenge properly, leaking oil on to the rear wheel. They had to make two pit stops to clean the oil before it cleared. The riders were ready to pack it in but the offer of prize money if they finished in the top six convinced them to continue. The bike was subsequently nicknamed *Slippery Sam*, and so began a legend and a history of racing success.

Success Home and Abroad

The Daytona 200-miler in the US presented a unique opportunity to influence sales with racing success against other leading manufacturers. New AMA National rules allowed 750cc OHV (overhead valve) and OHC (overhead cam) engines for road racing. Seeing the value of racing successes, Triumph USA contributed £30,000 to the factory development of the Triple racers. Seven bikes for practice week were constructed in just twelve weeks and shipped directly to Daytona from the UK.

The scene was set for a race like no other. Team Hansen fielded four Honda CB750s with Dick Man on their riders list. Cal Rayborn joined the fray on a new Harley XRTT along with the best 350 and 500 two-strokes from Yamaha, Kawasaki and Suzuki.

Son of Sam, a purposeful and effective race machine.

In this charged atmosphere the Triples looked like the ones to beat. The new Triples combined innovative and proven technology in a stunning, professional package. All seven bikes had a special Rob North frame cocooned in a BSA fairing designed using the Royal Aircraft Establishment (RAE) wind tunnel. The bikes were identical except for the colour scheme – blue/white for Triumph and red/white for BSA – with upright or sloping cylinders as on the road versions. They also used a five-speed Rod Quaife gearbox – an upgrade that caused some controversy as the road bikes were four-speeders. Cunningly, Doug Hele had sent fifty Quaife boxes to the US to be catalogued for sale, which made them legal for AMA racing.

Other upgrades included three 13/16th Amal GP carburettors, a 250-mm leading-shoe front brake and a 9-inch hydraulic rear disc brake.

Although the race was won by Dick Mann on a Honda, the Triples performed very well, with Gene Romero setting the fastest speed trap speed of 166.5 mph – not bad for a road-based design. In qualifying Romero set the fast lap time average of 157.34 mph, using a ribbed front tyre on the rear inflated to 75 lbs psi. The rear wheel with the ribbed tyre was kept in the boot of his car until all the other riders had left the pits so they did not see what he was doing. This reduced contact with the asphalt and thereby minimised rolling resistance. Romero said that riding the oval was very intimidating and that at speed it was like you were riding straight into a wall.

It was on the road racing circuits of the world that the battling Triples made the biggest impact, inflicting defeats and vanquishing the opposition to become the most successful production racer of all time, and in 1971 they would really flower.

Encouraged by their good performance in the Daytona failure, upgrades and improvements continued to be introduced by the Experimental Department as they prepared for the 1971 season. A new contact breaker assembly prevented ignition timing from wandering.

The Triples look so right in their road-racing guise, regardless of the paint scheme.

Many Triple owners ride the same bike on the road and on the track.

The steering head angle was changed along with the addition of a Rob North frame. The oil cooler was relocated to the nose of the fairing and twin discs replaced the Fontana front brake. The weight remained at 370 lbs but it was more powerful with 84 bhp at 8,500 rpm. It handled better as well as being more reliable and durable.

1971 saw the Triples dominate home and abroad, slaughtering opposition wherever they met it. The new bikes could be easily identified by the introduction of a front slot (the letter box) in the fairing nose which directed air to the oil cooler.

Daytona came around again with a real chance of reversing the failure of the previous year. Six bikes from earlier had remained in America and four new bikes were taken over. For the whole of practice and race week the Triples dominated. Paul Smart qualified fastest and Triples took the first three places. Dick Mann won on a BSA, followed by Gene Romero and Don Edme. Paul Smart's bike holed a piston while holding a 26-second lead. After the race the winning bike disappeared into the vastness of America.

Back home the victories just kept coming as the Tridents dominated the short circuits, winning the British 750cc Championship and the Superbike championship. Paul Smart won three of the six-leg Anglo-American Match Races. The other three were won by Ray Pickrell, as was the Thruxton F750 200-miler. Tony Jefferies was victorious in two rounds of the Superbike series and completed the F750 TT with an average of 102.85 mph.

By far the most famous race of 1971 was John Copper's success at Mallory Park's Race of the Year, piloting his BSA Triple. Doug Hele was not keen on providing a bike for John

but BSA management had promised the ride so he had no choice. The BSA rider was seen as no threat to world champion Giacomo Agostini on his all-winning 500cc MV Grand Prix Triple. During a close race in front of a massive crowd Cooper recovered from a major slide at 'The Esses' bend to win by 0.6 seconds. Two weeks later John Cooper repeated the medicine at Brands Hatch to etch his name in the annals of bike racing mythology.

Above and left: John Cooper's successful BSA Triple, on which he beat Giacomo Agostini on his MV, first at Mallory Park then in a second victory at Brands Hatch.

The Claiming Incident

During a year full of notable events, one event in the US nearly turned into Triumph's *annus horribilis.*

It was October 1971 at the Ontario Motor Speedway, 40 miles east of LA on the San Bernadino Freeway. John Cooper was rounding out a fabulous year with victory in the prestigious Champion Spark Plug 250 Mile Classic on his unbeatable BSA Rocket 3.

To create a level playing field and to discourage the major factories from using exotic designs that were beyond the resources of the private racer, they had the 'Claiming Rule'.

This 'Claiming Rule' allowed any finisher in a race to place a bid for the winning bike. It was with this background that unknown rider Bob Bailey stepped forward to exercise his right to bid for the winning BSA Rocket 3, placing a £1,000 ($2,500) bond to validate and support his claim.

This caused quite a stir because Doug Hele placed the value of the bike at £10,000 at least. John Copper's mechanic Steve Brown, whose skill had kept the Rocket 3 running like clockwork all season, and who had nurtured it during the 420 miles of practice and racing, now faced a new role. Steve had bonded with this machine and nobody was going to move it. He held on to the BSA, ready to repel all comers with a hide hammer in his hand.

Doug Hele and Bob Bailey went to have a private discussion. It was pointed out to Bob that some of the parts of the bike 'might be difficult to obtain'. Bob settled for the Triple raced by Tony Jeffries, which was despatched to him in 1971.

The same AMA rule also came to the fore at Pocono Raceway in Pennsylvania. This time it was frustrated US dealer Jim Cotterman from Freeport, Illinois, who demanded Gene Romero's winning 1971 Trident for his $2,000 bond, although his claim was rejected on a technicality. Jim was annoyed that he could not buy a machine with the Rob North frame, but he was kept happy by eventually being supplied with a 1970 Triple from US Equip.

148
112
60
120
26
SHOEI
Paul
THREE BEARS
RACING

130
DRESDA
TRIDENT
130
TRIDENT

Above and opposite: Over fifty years after their launch, Triples are still gracing race circuits around the world. This is a machine that is basically a road motorcycle and still beats all comers.

148

Racing Machines

The race team toured South Africa in 1972, when again the Tridents came up against Agostini and his MV. At Pietermaritzburg Paul Smart and Ray Pickrell had a substantial lead over Ago when Smart fell on the oil-covered track. Unfortunately, he took out Pickrell, who broke his collarbone and chipped a vertebrae.

At the second meeting, at the Kyalami Circuit, Smart finished second to Ago. This marked his final swan song, as he then switched to US team Hansen Kawasaki.

At the Imola Daytona-style 200-mile F750 race, Pickrell finished fifth and Tony Jefferies sixth. Percy Tait failed to finish when his rear magnesium hub collapsed. The race was won by a V-Twin Ducati.

Now the writing was on the wall, as for the first time the Experimental Department at Triumph didn't have a race shop. Management decided that Ray Pickrell would not be allowed to race his 1971 TT-winning Triple. However, Les Williams and some of his colleagues used his home as a race shop and secretly prepared the bike for Ray. This was the bike that had become known as *Slippery Sam*. The secret duo won the Silverstone Production Race, beating Percy Tait on a Rocket 3.

Les Williams bought the bike at the end of the season and rebuilt it with a lighter frame. *Slippery Sam* was then entered in and won a further three successive Production TTs.

It is the convention today that championship-winning riders will often be gifted the winning bike by their team. However, if successful Triple riders wanted their race machines, they had to buy them.

Paul Smart paid £1,000 for his lap record-winning Trident. Percy Tait and John Copper paid a similar amount for their Triples.

There is substantial ambiguity regarding information about the race machines, but it is generally agreed that there were eight 'Highboys' and eight 'Lowboys'. Each factory racing

Above and opposite: The closure of Meriden spelled the end for production of Triumph motorcycles. BSA had ceased production earlier and sadly the writing was on the wall. The Triumph Twins had reached the limit of their development and with the right management decisions there could have been a massive future for the Triples. (Photographer Ken Spall, NZ)

Stocks at Triumph Motorcycles Meriden as at 19th December 1973.

	T150V	T140V	TR7V	TR7P	T120V	T100R	TR5T	T100D	Test	TOTAL
Development Area	2	6	1		3	1	2			15
Coseley Bldg	29	91	5	1	3	12		14		155
Yard	73	93	15		58	173		11		423
Garage	22	24			2	3				51
R/Road	78	192	1	2	31	24	25			353
Unfinished No.2. Works	3	18	4	2	101	2	2		1	133
Packed & Wrapped	294	328	4	30	699	69	148			1572
TOTALS	5ol	752	30	35	897	284	177	25	1	2702

Total Machines still to strip and pack 1130

SHORTAGES :- Tank. 208 Machines Packed without Petrol Tanks.
Silencer Clips 106 Machines Packed without Silencer Clips.
Both items to hand.

Triple was built individually by skilled fabricators and engineers, and this is illustrated by the fact that each engine plate was specific in form and style to a particular machine and could not be transferred between bikes. So rather like the stripes on a zebra, a racing Triple can be identified by its engine plates. Of the sixteen race machines, the following information identifies twelve:

Eight Highboys, 1970

#1 Triumph, Percy Tait
#3 American team BSAs, riders being Mike Hailwood, Jim Rice, David Aldana
#6 American team Triumphs, riders being Gary Nixon, Gene Romero, Don Castro
#8 Triumph, Paul Smart as first rider

Eight Lowboys, 1971

#1 BSA, first ridden by Hailwood at Daytona, then Ray Pickrell back in UK – re-framed after crash at Oulton Park
#2 BSA, Dick Mann
#3 Triumph, Paul Smart
#4 Triumph, Gene Romero
#5 Triumph, Percy Tait
#6 Triumph, Tony Jeffries – this bike was sold to Bob Bailey following a claiming rule use against Cooper's BSA at Ontario
#7 BSA, John Cooper
#8 Triumph, Tony Jeffries – this was Jeffries' replacement bike after his was sold to Bob Bailey.

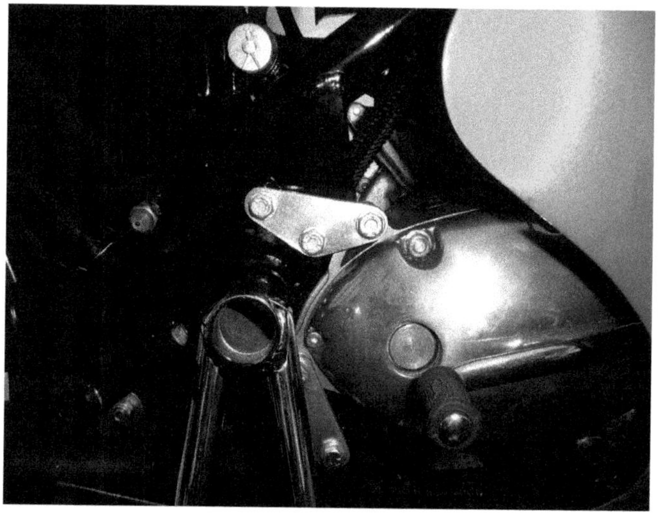

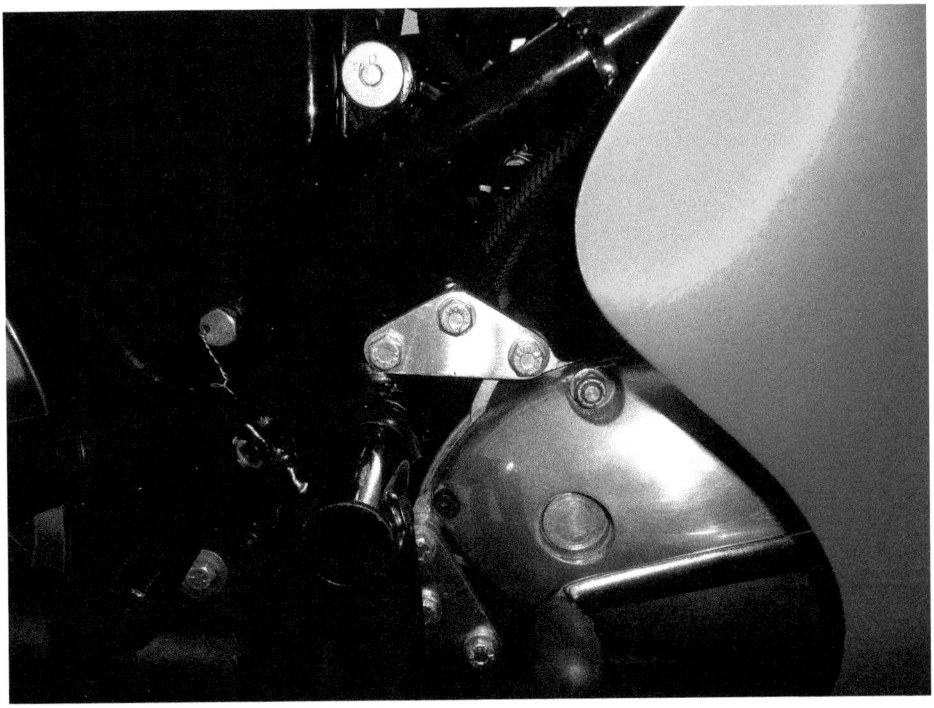

Above and opposite: Every racing Triple was hand-built by expert engineers and fabricators, and was individual. To illustrate this, these photographs of engine plates on racing Triples show they were each unique and could be identified like fingerprints or zebra stripes.

Comparison of Prototype and Production Hurricane

Left and opposite:
The original Hurricane created by Craig Vetter is substantially different from the X75 launched by Triumph. Take some time to compare the Vetter 3 (Hurricane Prototype) with the production model.

X·75

750cc

The history of the Triples is enhanced by a varied range of silencer designs. The 'Ray Gun' silencer started the trend for unusual designs.

The Hurricane X75 (TRX75) was based on the BSA Rocket 3 as they hoped to have an Americanised bike to beat Triumph in the US marketplace. However, by the time it was ready for launch BSA had gone out of business so it was launched under the Triumph name. The Rocket 3 was the last new model produced by BSA.

Model Development and Upgrades

The first P1 prototype Triple had a very different exhaust arrangement to that we see on production models. The centre exhaust pipe was very short, going directly into the cross pipe.

1969 Models (C Year Code)

Production started with the Rocket 3 in July 1968, with both the engine and frame as number 00101 – the lowest production number used. The use of the month and year code was not introduced until September 1968, so early machines do not carry the new security coding. As engines were assembled they were stamped with a sequential number. When the engine was randomly taken from the store, the engine number was stamped onto the frame, while the month and year code were added to the frame and engine number. Trident frames were stamped on the left side of the steering lug, while the Rocket 3 frames received the number on the left front engine mount lug. Construction continued for the Rocket's 1969 model year through to vehicle number GC03223, which was the final 1969 model year bike.

Production of the Trident mirrored the BSA machines, with production beginning at the start of July 1968, also with engine number 00101. Production continued to July 1969, with the highest number being DC04077, which was recorded as an experimental department racing machine.

The most successful racing engine of all time, still winning races fifty years after the launch of the road-going Triples. This was amazing success for an engine designed for the road and raced to improve motorcycle sales.

Production of the 1969 models should have commenced after the holiday shutdown in August 1969 but this did not happen. Production was delayed for nine months until April 1970 because of a number of in-service and production problems compounded by large unsold stocks in the US. The factory concentrated on production of Twins and Singles, and the production of Triples was suspended.

Above and below: A Triple-engined outfit competes in the Tuareg Rallye, piloted by John Young. The passenger is his son, also John.

Today enthusiasts attempt to push the envelope of Triple endeavour. A Triple-engined race car is one of those enthusiastic attempts.

1970 Models (D Code)

Production of the 1970 bikes started slowly and erratically between April 1970 and October 1970, with only 137 Rocket 3s (although a range of 240 numbers was used) and 287 Tridents being constructed. In truth the 1970 Trident model actually consisted of unsold 1969 specification models. Numbers again started at 00101, with the highest BSA being 00340, while its Triumph brother went from DD00101 to ED00388.

Sales of road models still needed a push, so in an effort to improve sales Triumph produced a 'beauty kit', which basically gave the Trident the familiar look of the original in-house design before Ogle were involved. The kit consisted of tank, mudguards, seat, side panels, exhaust pipes and oil cooler mountings. This was offered free of charge not only to new customers, but anyone who bought a Triple from 1 January 1970.

Given the original look of the Triples, this late T160 really is the swan from an ugly duckling.

Above, opposite and overleaf: Do Triples reflect the personality of the rider? Well they certainly vary depending on the skill and vision of the producer. I wonder if there are any original Triples anywhere?

RESERVED
TRIUMPH
TRIDENT
TRIUMPH
RENEGADE

144
145
TRIUMPH
bepi koelliker
TRIDENT
Castrol

1971 Models (E Code)

BSA's Umberslade Hall exercised a major influence over the much-revised 1971 models. The first Rocket 3 was built on 6 November 1970 with the engine number 00101. This was a show bike and appeared at the launch event in London and went on to be tested in the first edition of *Bike* magazine. Despite this early appearance, production of the 1971 models did not commence until January 1971 and continued to August 1971. For the Rocket 3 the highest engine number was 01193 and some of the later built bikes had the 1972 specification, which included the colour change to burgundy from firecracker red.

Because there was a need for racing homologation, 200 were built with the five-speed Quaife-type gearbox in February 1971.

In July 1971, US magazine *Cycle* welcomed the new beauty kit: 'The big 750 has lost its funny clothes and added an optional 5 speed transmission. Result? A Triumph looking Trident that does quarter mile dashes in 12.9. Easy'

The same magazine also carried an advert for the iconic movie *On Any Sunday*, a Bruce Brown film starring Steve McQueen that was to be launched that summer.

The T160 and rider are equally at home on the road as on the race circuit.

The 1971 and 1972 T150 adopted the more modern-looking bodywork and cycle gear from the new oil-in-frame Bonneville and TR6 lines launched in 1971. These included those new conical hubs front and rear, new front forks and rear shocks, a new headlight and mounting, a new gauge package and more. The new look truly transformed the bike, giving it a much more modern air. The 8-inch conical TLS front brakes on the '71 models were weak due to poor geometry on their actuator arms, but this was remedied by '72. Starting in 1972, some five-speed gearboxes were available as an option. The Trident did not get an oil-bearing frame like the Twins.

As 1971 progressed the impact of the Triple became ever greater in the UK. Owners changed the rear sprocket from 52T to a 62T. Changing the gearbox from a 19 to 17 saw a decrease in top speed but a vastly improved acceleration rate.

1972 Models (G Code)

BSA hit the ground running with production of the 1972 models. With often-seen number 00101, production started in August 1971. Production of bikes with the burgundy paint scheme with a black frame reached number 00643 with a smooth run until April 1972. Most Rockets had the four-speed gearbox; however, two were fitted with the five-speeds and the last bike despatched in May 1972 was a five-speeder (engine number 00641).

Trident production had a more tortuous route, with the first T150 1972 model being built in August 1971 (number JG00101). In their regal purple livery, an increasing number were fitted with the five-speed gearbox. Production rolled on until October 1972, ending with NG04777.

1973 Models (H Code)

There was no production of the BSA Rocket 3 in 1973 as BSA had ceased to exist as a motorcycle manufacturer, mainly due to the ineffectual leadership of Dennis Poore. Therefore, the Triples built for 1973 had their engines assembled at Small Heath, while the bikes themselves were constructed at Meriden.

Despite the demise of the Rocket, Triumph were still able to offer two models to customers for 1973: the Trident and the newly introduced Hurricane.

The first 'Vetter-designed' Hurricane X75 was built during September 1972, with Trident construction commencing in December of that year. The model was marked by the introduction of a disc front brake and modified silencer and carburation to comply with noise and emission restrictions in the US.

The numbering regime became a little confusing, with the first Hurricane picking up the number 00101 and the Tridents starting with number 00307, which followed Hurricane number 00306. The Hurricane reached no higher than number 02797, while the Trident production continued with the following numbers. The final 1973 machine was built on 6 September 1973 with the number 06040.

The next major model change came for the 1973 and 1974 T150V and this was the addition of a much-needed hydraulic front disc brake and the long-awaited five-speed gearbox, which is what the 'V' stands for in the model designation. Styling was cleaned up also, in keeping with the Bonneville line. The workers' strike then closed the Meriden plant early in 1974, cutting '74 Bonneville and TR7 production to little more than a trickle. But Tridents were built in BSA's Small Heath factory, so production went on unabated. It was not long before Triumph had ceased to exist as a company, along with its parent company BSA, being replaced by the worker-owned Meriden Co-operative, who were strapped for cash from the very start.

The Meriden Co-operative often didn't have enough money to pay for the parts needed to finish a shipment of bikes, so bikes didn't get shipped, orders didn't get filled, the money from those sales didn't come in and the Co-op's situation worsened by the day. So, even though they were free to build Tridents at Small Heath, unfettered by the worker lockdown, they had neither the money to build them nor the customers to sell them to. Despite all this, the dedicated Triumph men had one more trick up their sleeves for the Trident.

1974 Models (J Code)

The Trident T150V was the sole Triple for 1974, with construction of the Hurricane ending in January 1973.

June 1973 saw the start of 1974 model production, with number GJ40101 abandoning for this model year the usual start number of 00101. The motivation behind this move is not clear but could have been because 1973 model bikes were still being built, utilising the stock of engines with 1973 code numbers.

1975

1975 was the last year of Trident production and led to the best Trident ever: the T160. It finally got an electric start and a left-hand gear change. It had more of the look of the BSA Rocket 3 with forward-slanting barrels, which were introduced to accommodate the electric starter.

The new bike was dubbed the T160 in keeping with Triumph's convention of naming its highest-performance bikes with a 'T' for 'Triumph', followed by a theoretical top speed. The reasoning was that if a 650cc T110 Tiger was supposed to do 110 mph, then the new twin-carb 650cc Bonneville should be good for 120 mph, and therefore was a T120. When the Twin was pushed out to 750cc, it made sense that it should become a T140. In truth 140 mph from a 1973 Bonneville was a little optimistic. So it naturally followed that this new triple-cylinder superbike must logically be faster than the old Twins. Therefore, the model prefix was T150, thereby announcing to the world in Triumph code that the new Trident was a 150 mph motorcycle. While there is no record of the attainment of these speeds, it had a nice ring to it. Imagination over fact prevailed and with this awesome new Trident it only made sense that it must take on an even more ambitious name: the Triumph Trident T160.

Esso
PLUS

TRIDENT

TRIUMPH

TRIUMPH

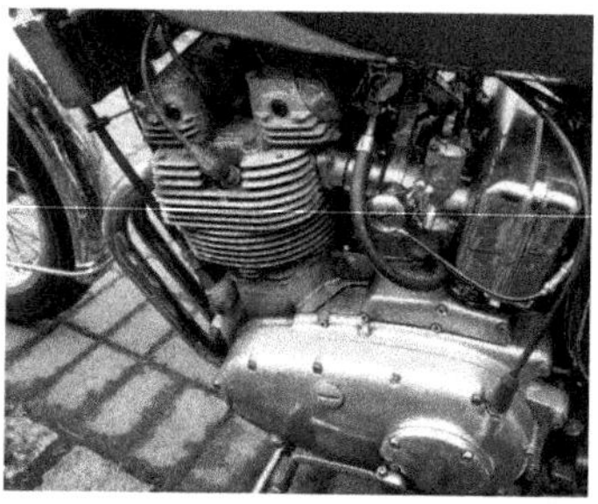

The Triumph Trident T160 – the ultimate development of the Triple. An electric start, a forward-tilted engine and the 'Vetter Top Line' make this bike the ultimate road Triple.

The Triple has been the basis for many novel creations; this 'Double Triple' six-cylinder engine is in early development, and is seen here at an auto jumble.

1976 Triumph Cardinal

One of the last batches of 288 Triples were destined for Australia, with another 224 for the US. However, Norton Villiers Triumph (NVT) diverted them from those markets (where they faced almost impossible competition from the big four Japanese manufacturers) to meet an order of Tridents for the Saudi Arabian police force. Police forces in the UK had, for the most part, switched to BMW motorcycles, but some like Yorkshire had been using Tridents. Five shipments, totalling 450 bikes, were sent to Saudi Arabia. Another 130 were still in the UK when the Saudis cancelled the order in early 1977. In response, NVT decided to sell them on the home market as the Triumph Cardinal.

At the time the list price of a stock T160 – if you could find one! – was £1,211 (inc. VAT), with most dealers listing them for £1,198. The accessories were worth about £150 – including crash bars, spot lamps, air horns, tri-point screen, panniers, a single seat and radio rack. NVT listed the Cardinal for £1,522.80 (inc. VAT).

The weekly paper *Motorcycle News* even had a 'Mark the Ball' competition with a Cardinal as the prize.

Interest in Triples grew to the extent that people wondered what happened to the 450 bikes sent to Saudi Arabia, which made up about 6.25 per cent of the total production of just over 7,000 T160s.

The Cardinal – a world-travelled T160 returning home for sale.

The introduction of twin disc front brakes was a major improvement in bringing this substantial vehicle to a halt.

Dealers in the UK began bringing the bikes back in the early 1980s, restoring and reselling them, usually in standard T160 spec. Returning machines had incredibly low mileage – sometimes no more than a couple of hundred miles! However, they were much abused and, as might be expected, were totally encrusted in sand, with desert dust everywhere.

The Quadrant

The Triumph Quadrant was designed and built by Doug Hele in 1973. It was a 1,000cc four-cylinder motorcycle made from Trident parts (although the camshaft was sourced outside the factory). The fourth cylinder resulted from grafting an extra mid-crankcase unit; since the primary chain case and final drive sprocket could not be moved, the fourth cylinder protruded from the right side of the bike.

Why Hele developed this machine is unknown, since the lopsided design could never compete with Japanese motorcycles such as the Honda CB750 or the Kawasaki Z1. An inside view is that Hele's efforts were a waste of resources that, with NVT's precarious finances, should have been directed to marketing the 900cc Triple Thunderbird III.

Above and below: The original Quadrant prototype bike. Sadly, it never went into production as the means did not really exist and the competition was too strong. The Quadrant can be viewed at the National Motorcycle Museum, Solihull, along with twenty-five Triples.

Trident T180 – Thunderbird 111

During 1975 an NVT prototype 900cc Triple, the T180, rose from the drawing board, but the hapless NVT management failed to proceed to production. In a cynical move the prototype was transferred to the Meriden Co-operative, without any corresponding funds to support further development. Despite experimenting with the T180 engine in an oil-bearing frame, the Thunderbird 111 did not make it to production.

The T180 (otherwise known as the P76, which in production was to be named the Thunderbird 111) was started by NVT at Kitts Green in 1975 with a view to building a stopgap big-bore motorcycle out of existing parts, seeing as the British motorcycle industry was on its knees at the time. Three 870cc engines were produced: 001 in an Isolastic frame, 002 in a standard frame, and 003 as a spare engine. Although looking identical to the standard T160 engine, these engines were long stroke, 870cc, and used in-line contact rocker boxes, as used on the works racers. None of the crankcases, barrels or heads were interchangeable with a standard T160 engine as the barrel stud arrangement was spaced further apart.

From speaking to people who have ridden a T180, the top speed was similar to the T160, but the extra 129cc gave it much superior low-down torque. During the year Les Williams and Steve Brown prepared a racing machine housed in an ex-Ray Pickrell Lowboy chassis with the T180 high-performance engine of 871.14cc. Engine 003 was fitted with works cams (TH13 inlet, TH6 exhaust), a lightweight clutch/primary drive and other works parts, producing 91.1 bhp at 8,500 revs.

Piloted by Dave Croxford, the T180 racer ran in the 1,000cc race at the 1975 British Grand Prix at Silverstone and finished sixth. After the Silverstone race the engine was stripped and the piston circlips were found to have come out due to excessive end float on the big ends, the barrel was scored and the piston rings were damaged!

The author had heard of the existence of a mythical big-bore Triple, but thought it might be legend rather than fact. However, I got to talk to Clive Blake, who had personal experience of this mythical beast:

> My first experience with the T180 came in 1980 I believe, when a friend of mine Terry Allwood owner of Hastings Motorcycles in East Sussex phoned to tell me he

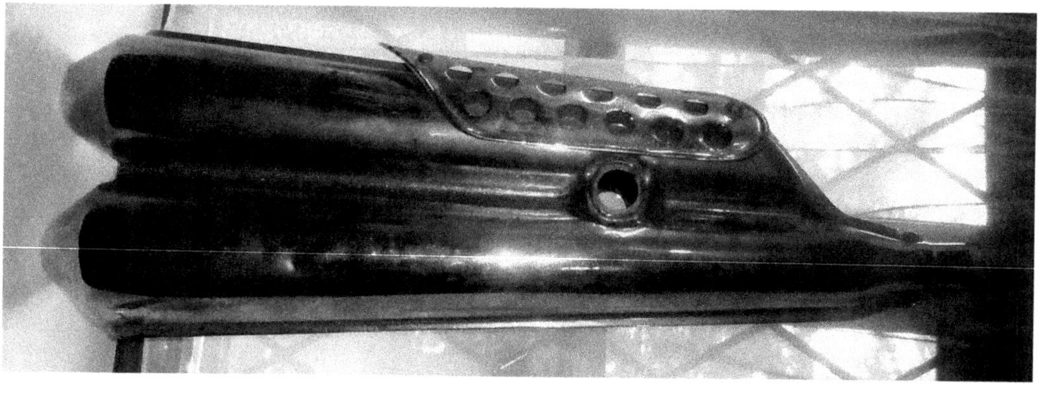

The silencers from the T180 – another missed opportunity.

had bought a Triumph Trident prototype T180 motorcycle and some engines from the then NVT Shenstone HQ in Staffordshire.

On arrival I was confronted by what looked like a standard T160 with Thunderbird 111 decals on the side panels, to say I was disappointed would be an understatement, but on closer inspection I noticed the rocker box arrangement was different (line contact rockers) and it had T180 002 stamped on the drive side crankcase. I was asked if I wanted to take it out for a ride but in all honesty I couldn't be bothered, a decision I was later to regret.

Clive also observed a spare T180 engine numbered T180 001. This engine looked like it had been modified quite a bit as the front engine mount had been cut away and re-welded, and the centre exhaust port had a spigot welded in similar fashion to the T150.

The complete T180 had apparently been restored by Les Williams for someone at NVT when Les worked from home in Coventry, and the engine had been overhauled by Steve Brown (owner of T180 engine 003).

Some twenty years later Clive purchased the T180 001 prototype engine he had seen before. The engine was authenticated by Les Williams and then sat in Clive's garage for few years before being loaned to Bill Crosby for display at the London Motorcycle Museum.

Ridden on the road and on the track – a legend.

Above and opposite: To mark the 50th anniversary of the Triples, a year-long 50-50 Challenge was organised with the added aim of raising funds for the Donna Louise Trust charity. Here challengers visit Kitts Green, where the Triple was designed, and what is left of the BSA factory. The book was used to record the completion of the challenges and over £17,000 was raised for DLT.

B S A
RF18 FON

50 Years - 50 Challenges
50-50
Triumph Trident / BSA Rocket 3
50th Anniversary of the Triples 1968 - 2018
The Donna Louise
Children's Hospice

Machine Numbering System

The numbering system for motorcycles allows the bike to be tracked and is used to confirm the age and originality of the machine. Today, proof of numbers is very important if you want an age-related registration number – for instance, if the bike has been re-imported from abroad.

From their early days Triumph had had a numbering system that was logical and effective, giving both the engine and frame the same number. As ever BSA had a system that was more complicated than it needed to be, with no relationship between the frame and engine numbers.

Triple owners can be confused by the identification of the model year. The system used by BSA and Triumph was supposed to coincide with the factory shut-down for the summer holiday fortnight. On their return from their annual break workers would find the factory cleaned, re-fitted and supplies of new parts, colours and specifications for the following

Above and left: Engine and frame numbers should match, which was the Triumph system.

QUADRANT
Triumph's ill-fated four

John Kerr looks at another British prototype that bit the dust.

PHOTOGRAPHY RICHARD ADAMS

The Quadrant as restored by the National Motorcycle Museum. The machine was originally built as a feasibility study, and was not intended to enter production in this form.

LOOKING back over the last decade, one thing is clear: Britain's large-scale motorcycle industry did not perish for want of design ideas. Ten years ago, the visionary Bert Hopwood was getting ready to present to the BSA-Triumph board his remarkable plans for a modular range from a 200cc single through 400cc twins and 600cc triples to a ripsnorting one litre V5. With the right investment, this 138mph flagship could have leap-frogged the Honda fours to pip today's V-multis to the market by years.

But only weeks before that board meeting, BSA-Triumph crashed. Merged into NVT, the modular designs never saw the light of day. Down in the workshops, however, Doug Hele and his experimental team were working on a number of promising projects in the metal: a four-valve-head Commando, a 500cc twin-cam parallel twin, a Commando with a unique balancing device. And there was a stream of Trident derivatives: a single-overhead-cam version; a two-up, one-down crank for smoother running; a Trident with Isolastic engine mounting; the 900cc T180 triple; and even a four-cylinder 1,000cc derivative called logically enough, the Quadrant.

If many of these developments had inherent engineering appeal, it was the Quadrant that would have had substantial market potential. To the others' icing it would have been a completely new cake, the first one-litre British bike since the demise of the big Vincent in 1955 and the Ariel Square Four in 1960. It could have provided lively competition for the Kawasaki Z1, which had already seen off Honda's 750cc fours, and opened up the starting gates for the hyperbike stampede. With its across-the-frame configuration and 1,000 cubes the Quadrant would have been a fitting contender for the race.

But it was not the Honda and Kawasaki fours that NVT was inspired to follow. Doug Hele had come back from the Isle of Man in 1974: 'I'd seen these Yamaha fours racing so well that I got to thinking', he says. 'I'd never been happy with the exhaust note of the two-up, one-down Trident; it always sounded like a four-cylinder car engine missing on one, and frequency-wise that's just what it was. Then it dawned on me that we could put on another cylinder.'

Ex-drag racer and sprinter Norman Hyde, who then worked under Hele at Kitt's Green, Birmingham, recalls: 'When it came out in 1969, the Trident was the last word in sophistication and smoothness. But by 1974 the American dealers were griping about its vibration compared to the Jap fours.'

Hele assembled a top-secret 'inner sanctum' of workers for the Quadrant: himself, experimental shop foreman Alan Barrett and Jack Shemans, a brilliant engine specialist and the man who'd assembled the winning motors for three Daytona 200s. They first struck a blow on the Quadrant in June 1974, working in such secrecy that neither the rest of the experimental team nor management — including chairman Dennis Poore — knew the project existed.

But the machine was never a pre-production prototype and therefore never underwent performance and durability trials. The construction route was not intended to be the definitive method of volume manufacture. The Quadrant — only one was made — was simply an exercise to see if the idea of a four was feasible.

The bottom end was where work kicked off. The crankcase posed few problems; to the Trident's three-piece crankcase — a centre plus two outer covers — was added another centre to give five main bearings. Outer covers stayed the same. The crankshaft proved rather more testing. Hele took the three-piece two-up, one-down crank then being tried out on an experimental Trident and added another piece. The whole four-section flat crank was spigoted and dowelled and pressed together. In volume production, this would have been impractical — a simple

33

The Quadrant has caught the imagination of motorcyclists despite never reaching production.

year's products in place and ready for construction to commence. This enabled new models to be in dealers' showrooms in preparation for the selling season. The bulk of the new model year production in the autumn was consigned to the huge US market. The UK selling market was condensed into the spring and summer and was met by production in the early spring.

As the summer of 1968 approached, worldwide concern grew at fraud related to new motorcycles. The solution to improve security and traceability was the use of identification stamping that included the month and year the machine had been built. The coding would be supported by legally required written factory records of production. The new secure system was introduced in September 1968, just after the start of production of the 1969 (launch models) model year. To further diminish the possibility of fraud on stolen machines, the crankcases were modified by the inclusion of a raised pad with a rolled Triumph or BSA logo, on which was stamped the relevant number code.

Then, in 1969 BSA joined the Triumph factories and moved to use a common engine and frame numbering system. This reliable system was employed during the whole of the production run of the Tridents and Rocket 3s.

Thus, if you are trying to age either model you have a reliable system to confirm production details. Both engine and frame numbers comprise a model identifier, a two-character date code and a five-digit sequential serial number. The model identifier can

Own a Triple and travel the world!

appear at the start or end of the number sequence. The date code, however, always appears immediately before the five-digit serial number. This system ensures that every machine that left the factory had matching numbers.

As an engine was completed it was stamped with the five-digit sequential serial number by hand. The numbered engine would then be stored to await introduction to a frame. Once a rolling chassis was completed, an engine was drawn from the stores and married to the rolling chassis. This meant that engines used did not follow a numerical sequence. When the two came together the month and model year code were added, along with the model identifier.

Records indicate that the last shipment of BSA Triples went to the US in two batches on 1 and 2 November 1971. Another 200 bikes were subsequently built and shipped to various other markets. The last four bikes were despatched on 8 September 1972, prior to BSA closing their doors forever.

Development of the Triumph Triples continued with the T160s. Production for this model was commenced, as was the practice, in August of the preceding year (1974) and ran through to July 1975. In addition some were built in late 1975 and into early 1976. These bikes will have 'N' as the model year – even though there was no official 1976 model year for the T160. It is estimated that around 7,500 T160s were constructed over the model's production run.

As always, BSA were less than diligent with their numbering of the Rockets, with late 1971 engines being used for the early 1972 models.

The famous letter-box fairing improved air flow to cool the Triple engine during racing.

The NVT Easy Rider moped. When production of the Triple ended, it was replaced by the moped.

A lion in the jungle of classic British motorcycles.

The Triples were meant to be ridden and not stored in a shed. Both modern and classic events are the domain of these iconic motorcycles.

Percy Tait.

This publicity shot of the BSA Fury shows the influence of the Vetter top line.

Triple Numbering Convention

The numbering system for the Tridents is easy to follow once you have the code. This, of course, assumes that there was no human error in the physical stamping of the numbers.

Letter	Month	Model Year
A	January	1979
B	February	1980
C	March	1969
D	April	1970
E	May	1971
G	June	1972
H	July	1973
J	August	1974
K	September	1975
N	October	1976
P	November	1977
X	December	1978

The first letter in the code indicates the month of manufacture, while the second letter refers to the model year of the motorcycle. Model years stared in August of the preceding year and ran through to July.

Therefore, a March 1969 bike would carry the code beginning CCxxxxx and shipping would have taken place in March 1969. Equally, with a November 1976 bike you would see a code beginning PNxxxxx.

A selection of historical racing Triples housed in the National Motorcycle Museum, Solihull. NMM is well worth a visit to see the finest display of British motorcycles in the world. Every year there is an open day when entry is free to all, so watch the news.

Triples remain competitive on circuits that never see a Honda CB 750.

Pretty in purple.

Above and opposite: Five different Triples in New Zealand with five different clock layouts. What is a standard Triple?

Above and left: Every Triple is a personal possession and long-term ownership is the norm. This Triple is owned by someone with a sense of humour as the bike is labelled 'Slippery Sid'. It was observed at the WATOC Rally of the Year organised by TOMCC NZ Inc in New Zealand during February 2019.

A replica tribute to the successful Bol d'Or 24 Hour Race.

Another P1 at the Stafford Show in 2018.

The badge of the 50-50 Triumph Trident/BSA Rocket 3: 50th Anniversary of the Triples 1968–2018. It is worn with pride by those that took up the challenge.

Triumph Trident T150 – 'The Best Production Racer Ever'.